I0143186

The Light of Faith

~

Poems and Plays

Grace Bourget

En Route Books and Media, LLC

Saint Louis, MO

⊕ENROUTE

Make the time

En Route Books and Media, LLC

5705 Rhodes Avenue

St. Louis, MO 63109

Contact us at contact@enroutebooksandmedia.com

Cover Credit: *Star of Bethlehem* by Edward Burne-Jones, 1890, edited by Grace Bourget. Interior Illustrations by Grace Bourget.

Copyright © 2023 by Grace Bourget

ISBN: 979-8-88870-057-0

Library of Congress Control Number: 2023940834

Dedication

To the Sorrowful Heart of Our Lady of Salette

&

The Holy Face of Jesus

~

For the intentions of those with bleeding hearts,

For those in need of the light of Faith and those who know its beauty,

&

For my friends who have been with me as I've drawn closer to the Light

of Faith, namely:

Kristopher,

Marija, Teresa, Christina,

and Chantal.

~

"It is so sweet to serve the good God in the dark night of trial; we have

this life only in which to live by faith." - St Thérèse of Lisieux.

~

"The birth, death, and resurrection of Jesus means that one day

everything sad will come untrue." - J.R.R. Tolkien.

Table of Contents

i

~

Poems

~

The Donkey

She came upon the snowy manger scene in the forest and
stopped to gaze into the stable. Her eyes fell upon the humble
donkey crouching beside the Infant King.

"You see . . . you're just like me, she murmured.
"The world calls you a fool,
A heartache's mistake,
A humble tool.
But you broke your back. . .
Carrying the One Who carried the Cross for love's lack."

She brushed her hand over the donkey's wooden nose.

"I guess I'm just . . .
I'm just the same.
You're very tame . . .
Without a name . . .
A beast of burden . . .
Always hurting . . ."

"Yet, you, the one God knew,
Stable to kingdom's tide.
No palace, gilded;
No stallion brave to ride-
Softness and trust, love;
Your meekness gently banded, safe as the snowy dove."

"Life's Companion;
But then our God,
The God of All,
Born very small-
Died on a Cross,
The devil's loss."

"Am I to share His scorn?
Brush away the snow-sting,
See Thee around me,
Through my imagining?
All at once, in view-
The starry flame of angelfire, scars of rainbow hues!"

"Dear donkey, know
We are Love's Thorn:
We mirror Him:
We let love win!
And then we'll see
Just what it means!"

"We needn't fear the thorn of man,
God suffered this upon His brow
We must love for Him alone,
And let the pain be our crown.
Sometimes, heartache holds the key.
Crossbearer, you see. . .mirror true, you're just like me."

Starlight Carol

A star is shining in the sky,
A tiny hand reaches for the light;
Two hearts beating,
A mother holds her Child tight.

Stars dance, His eyes light,
A baby's cry enters the night
Sweet little one, your star is dancing in the sky
Hush little one, go lullaby.

A tiny head lying on His Mother's heart,
Soon will be sorrow there, but joy is now!
Songs float down from on high.
Her soft melody and a kiss on His brow.

A baby born, so soon to die
Men sleep, and wonder why
The stars shine so bright;
An angel's voice echoes through the night.

Nails are coming soon, to lift up One so small;
But now is hope and peace for all;
Bathed in starlight!

Mary's Little Lamb

Intended as a Mother's Lullaby

Mary had her little Lamb, and I do, too;
Her's was Jesus, and mine is you.
For thirty years in a row, then,
Where'er Mary went, her Lamb was sure to go.

So the story went, wrapped up in a stable,
Beneath the burning, starry sky:
The Angels sang, the donkey brayed,
There, one cold, deep, December night,
The little snow-white Lamb was laid.

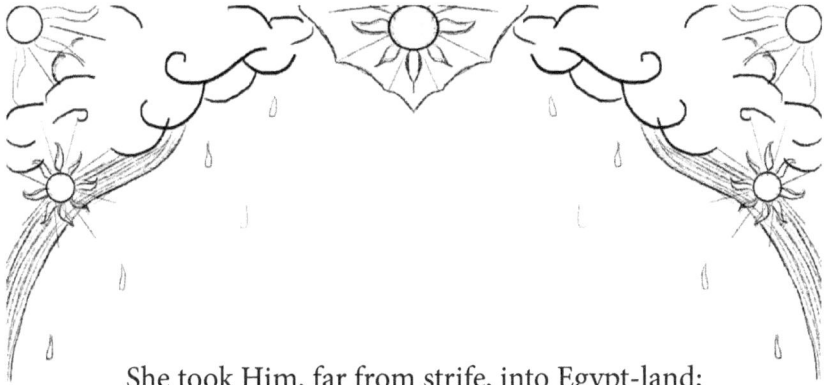

She took Him, far from strife, into Egypt-land;
Joseph worked, a carpenter-man,
Mary bore exile every day,
While Christ, Heaven's Light and Lamb, was there at
play.

Home at last, from far Egypt to Galilee,
Where lay sea of sapphire blue;
Jesus learned well His father's trade,
The rough-hewn wood was carved away;
And a shadowing Cross He made.

When time had come, into the desert He went,
Shade found the Lamb's Will couldn't be bent.
In Cana He made wine from water;
And the Lamb knew 'twas almost time for slaughter.

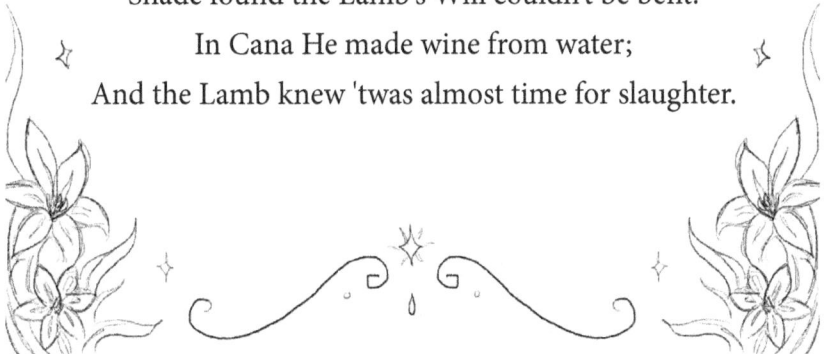

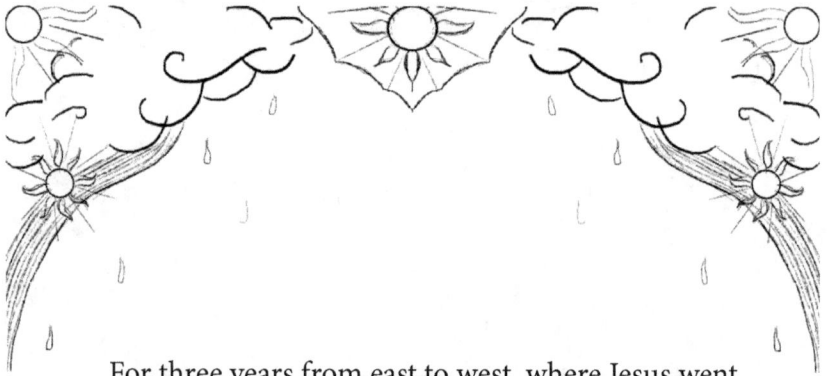

For three years from east to west, where Jesus went,
His Mother was sure to follow;
Love's heartbeat, comfort wouldn't borrow.
She saw His anguished offering,
Which pierced the Mother's heart with sorrow.

Fleece red-rose, the Lamb lay in her arms silent,
His face bathed by tears, her lament.
Closed in God's tomb, death died in agony
But did not allay the Mother's grief to see.

Spring sprang, one brilliant sunrise, the Lamb appeared!
All was hailed in glory-of-snow,
All pain's sorrow fallen away,
Broken tears were changed to life's dew,
Never again would dark night outlast the day.

While the Lamb ascended to His kingly throne,
Earthly vale never more to roam;
Our Mother remained to console
Beloved children who remained mourning below.

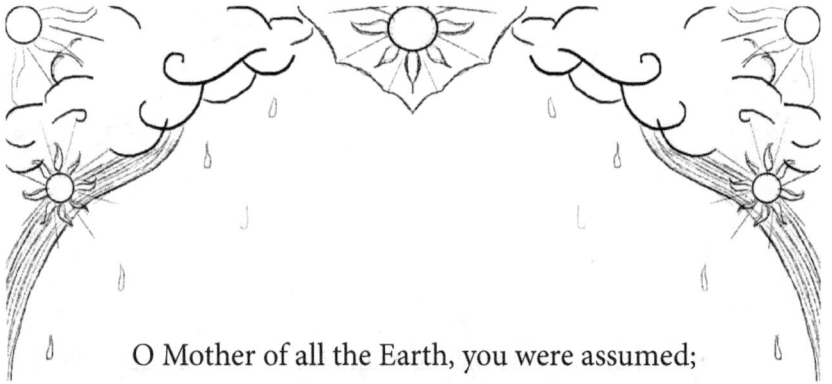

O Mother of all the Earth, you were assumed;
At last united with your Son,
A crown upon you was bestowed,
From man's crime came holy vict'ry;
Death by love, hope for all below.

From then on, deathless, the age-old story ran
How Mary had a little lamb,
From millennia, long ago,
Whose fleece, mantle of the just, was white as snow.

And so, my child, when you are grown,
Soon, loving, you will beg to know:
"Why does the Lamb love Mary so?"
Why, Mary loves her little Lamb, you know.

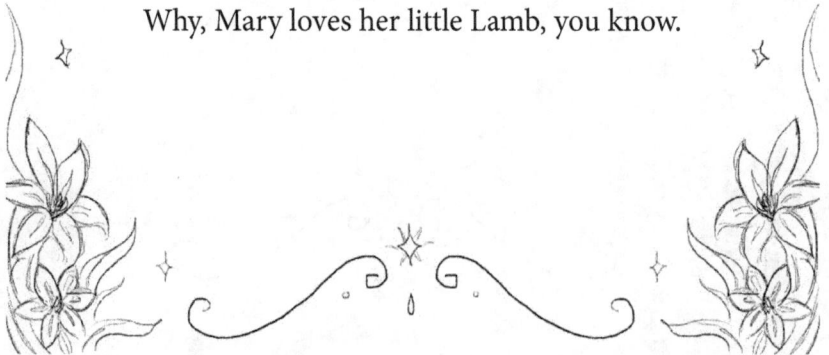

Hellebore

Hellebore, 'twas said of yore,
Was 'twixt Christmas and Lenten-tide
With Christmas snow and Lenten shade,
The love of Christ and His pain.

~

The whitened blossom,
Birthed in snow,
Tells of Christ's virgin birth,
His ever-purity.

…

Little lambs and gentle hands,
A Mother softly sighing.
Stars above, Heaven's love,
Shepherds and Kings a'falling.

~

But then this bright blossom's hue
Matured with Christ's own years,
Their birth the same, their lives the same,
Even the same own tears.

…

The Rose was blamed, put to shame,
Purpled with man's designs and heinous crimes.
Designs of pride, crimes of hate,
Against Christ's love, sent pain.

~

Bruised and beaten,
The purpled blossom
Birthed in sweat and blood,
Tells of Christ's unending love,
His thorny suffering.

….

Heavy bands and rough hands,
A people madly crying,
Dawn above, Heaven's love,
Who knew the walls were falling?

~

But then this tender blossom's petals
Crushed beneath Christ's own cross,
Their birth the same, their lives the same,
Even the same own tears.

....

Ruby blood, paths strewn with crushed rose-buds,
'Twixt Christmas beauty and Lenten-pain,
With Christmas light and Lenten sacrifice,
The Heart of Christ and His suffering.

~

The darkened blossom,
Bruised among the olives,
Tells of Christ's blameless suffering,
His ever-innocence.

....

Angry chants and tearing hands,
A Mother softly weeping,
Dark skies above, Heaven's love,
Heavy blows a'falling.

~

Hands were nailed, feet impaled,
Thorns enamored, petals bled,
The people were a'crying,
While the world's Breath lay dying.

....

And now this brave blossom's petals
Were bedewed with Christ's own Blood.
Their birth the same, their lives the same,
Even the same own tears.

~

A mother's sorrow, her strength the flower borrowed,
'Twixt crowd and Cross she stood.
With Christmas silence and Lenten veil,
She beheld God's suffering.

....

The purple blossom,
Bruised by blindness thorns,
Tells of Christ's loneliness,
His ever-longing Heart.

~

A last chance and bleeding hands,
A Mother silently standing,
Clouds above, Heaven's love,
Precious Blood a'falling.

…

She stood aside, no one heard her cry,
They alone saw her, smiling with a sigh
They welcomed her to stay.
For though that blossom was darker now,
Her sweetness was the same.

~

But then darkness fell upon the earth,
The Father's Will fulfilled.
God's cry her own, she fell with Him,
Living till the end.

…

The rain poured down, soaking the ground,
And washed her petals bright.
She raised her face, and with God's grace,
Became a reminder divine:

~

A white snowfall of purity,
To heal the ancient pain;
A purple shadow to remind
Of God enduring suffering.
The poison inside tells of God,
Who took the snakebite willingly
To heal our age-old agony.
The petals and the gold within
Tell us of Heaven's King.
He became a shepherd-boy,
Picking flowers for His Queen.

…

~

And now this graced blossom's lesson,
You have learned in time;
Your birth the same, your lives the same,
Even the same own tears.

. . .

Written for my friend Helen on her 21st birthday.

A Rose-Colored World

Wild roses are many in hue,
Yellow, green, rose-violet and red,
Yet never blue.

Some stand upon the mountains,
Some lie on the plains,
Some tint the forest,
Or carpet the garden ways.

Some blossoms are shyer,
Others are brighter,
Some sleep till morning,
Some sleep till the dark.
Some never waken.

But there are those that open to the sun,
Bright blossoms petals, bejeweled,
Every one.

A thousand rainbows in each raindrop,
A million worlds of life never seen,
The silence of dreams that have never been sung.

Each blossom different, some petals torn.
Some lie cushioned among thorns.
Some bear fruits all golden-red
Gold for the sun and red for the dead.
A rainbow of blossoms for all that's above,
Green the leaves for everlasting love.

Some men gather them as they adore.
Some maidens weave crowns for divine royalty,
Some Kings make of them crowns for their Queens.
Some Mothers heal children at sin's door.
Some maidens named Therese hold them close,
Vowing to drop them to those down below.
Some Princesses hide their gift-giving,
And their King's love brings holy wine from woe.

But what if I told you. . .
That there is a land,
Where roses meet stars and sky meets sea. . .
Where storms only rumble and never hold sway,

Streams are like jewels and ribbons of light;
The Queen of the Roses cradles her children,
And the King of the Thornbush raises
His Cross from men?

Here, no storms to drown them out,
Here 'tis love that ends the drought.
Would you believe it?
Wouldn't you see it?
On every rose bloom, a thousand reflections,
Broken dreams that have gone up to heaven?

~

Sweetest of the blossoms are those among thorns,

For no one is closer,

And no one is safer

Than she who is cradled by the Queen of the Roses,

And carried by the King of the Thorns.

~~

~

Written for Chantal on her 20th birthday.

~

Song of the Bleeding Heart

I asked the King of Heaven's heart,
Hide me within Thy lance-wound,
To bind me to Thy broken heart;
Hold me closer, 'till there is no room!

To hear His heartbeat's tune:
And like silver-flash of sunken moon,
I learned the love of His heart!

~

So many times I've loved him,
And had my heart broken in the rain,
But You gave me hope with him,
And asked my love to remain!

~

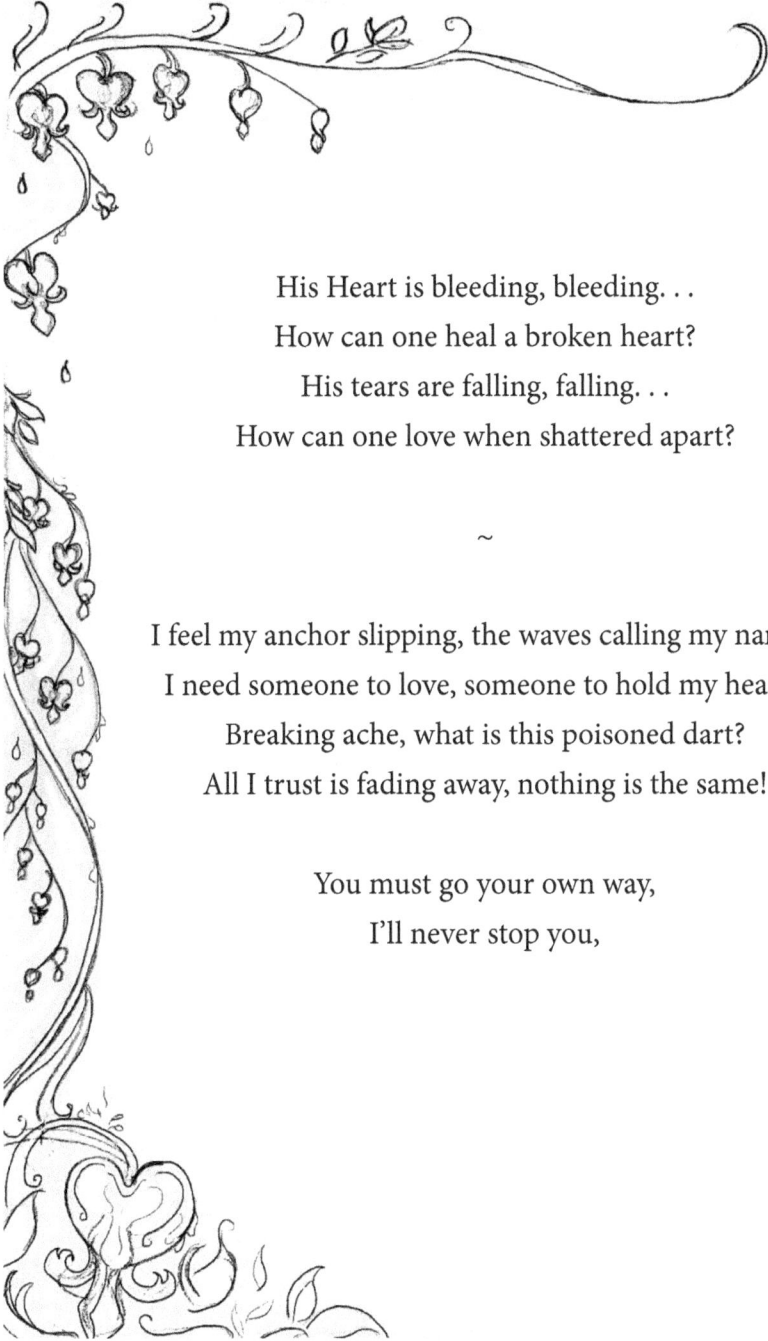

His Heart is bleeding, bleeding. . .
How can one heal a broken heart?
His tears are falling, falling. . .
How can one love when shattered apart?

~

I feel my anchor slipping, the waves calling my name -
I need someone to love, someone to hold my heart -
Breaking ache, what is this poisoned dart?
All I trust is fading away, nothing is the same!

You must go your own way,
I'll never stop you,

How do I know if my heart beats true,
When my only anchor was you?
Everyone says that I should let go,
But I fear that I don't know -

~

His Heart is bleeding, bleeding. . .
How can one heal a broken heart?
His tears are falling, falling. . .
How can one love when shattered apart?

~

Come back, He says, he's what you lack -
Love is unanswered pain, watered in the rain
Turned my heart back again,
Sewed the shatter, ripped and scattered,

As though never a cross so cruel, it mattered ,
All as was before, it was never a chore!
A heart renewed, never poisoned at the core!

~

I wish you knew what you mean to me:
That you're everything I'll ever be,
That it's God inside you Who I see,
That your heart holds my key -

I wish you knew I'd give you my everything,
You're the melody my heart sings,
You alone to be my earthly king!

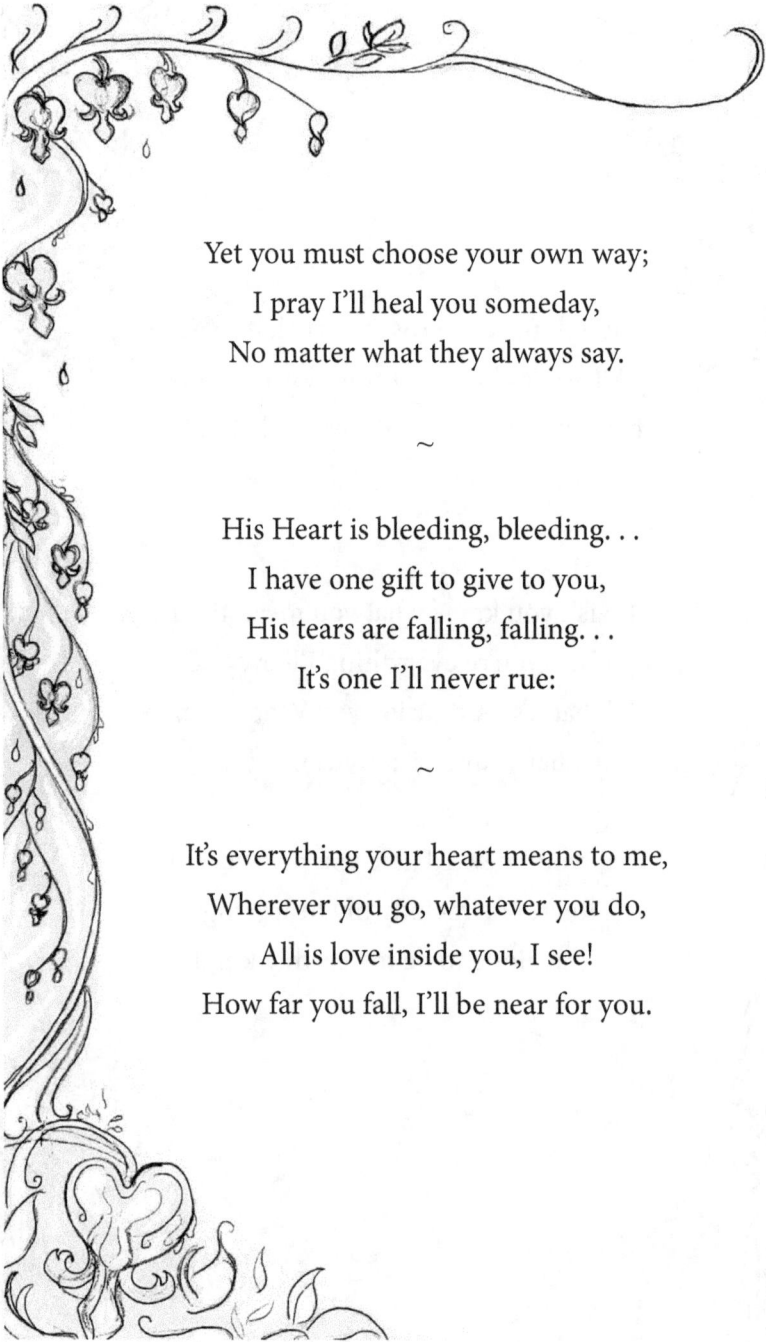

Yet you must choose your own way;
I pray I'll heal you someday,
No matter what they always say.

~

His Heart is bleeding, bleeding. . .
I have one gift to give to you,
His tears are falling, falling. . .
It's one I'll never rue:

~

It's everything your heart means to me,
Wherever you go, whatever you do,
All is love inside you, I see!
How far you fall, I'll be near for you.

You should see the stars that shine over your head,
The angels always calling your name,
You're everything He ever said.
Nothing will ever be the same!

Rainbows dancing through the sky-
You're like the sunshine in the rain!
Can you hear heaven's sigh?
And He's the balm in all my pain.

~

His tears are falling, falling. . .
This love that will never die-
Can you hear Him calling, calling?
Catching every tear from my eyes!

~

In the shadows of despair,
When you think no one cares,
When you need someone there,
If you can't come up for air -

When the world shuts you in,
When the world shuts you out,
Even in shadows of sin;
Never a shadow of doubt -

That five hearts long to hold you close,
Do you know just how dear?
Unfold in God's Heart like a rose,
If only you draw near!

~

His tears are falling, falling. . .
This love that will never die -
Can you hear Him calling, calling?
Catching every tear from my eyes!

~

If you need a path to get to Him,
And oh! If you need a stepping stone,
His mother's heart is waiting to let you in!
Proof that you aren't alone, our hearts never roam!

Precious Blood, wash over me,
Beating Heart, stay close to me,
Love of God that sets me free:
Draw me close, may he see Thee!

Let Him wash over you at midnight
When your heart fills with fright
Know we're at your side, holding you tight
You're in His Heart's pierced side

~

His tears are falling, falling. . .
This love that will never die-
Can you hear Him calling, calling?
Catching every tear from my eyes.

~

~

I asked the King of Heaven's heart,
Hide me within Thy lance-wound;
To bind me to Thy broken heart,
Hold me closer, 'till there is no room.

To hear His heartbeat's tune:
And like silver-flash of sunken moon
You gave me hope in him,
And so my love remains within!

Passion of Love

Between panes of crystal glass,
Wavering weave of blue-gold and shade,
Mist of morning dew and sunlight-ray;
Sea-silk and love, heart's repast,
Or, shiv'ring haste of death's pain?

Torment touched, blossoming grave,
Guilt and hope, flowering shame
Visage ever bewildering!
A Soul, only a breath, becoming
Silhouette of thundering!
Was ever anyone this brave?
Yet never were faces so the same!

Golden arrows, shooting stars,
Broken chains and twisted hearts!
Shadows of sin are flying;
Thou art all grace supplying!
Countenance of Holy Gold,
Passion of love yet untold!

Between now and ever, hearts are cast,
Errors, terrors flee before Thy Face;
Not long will the tempest rage,
May I crash, burn in Thy Heart's fire at last!
Whirling suns, galaxies, draw me in!

~~

Holy Face of Heaven's Light,

Keep within our hearts tonight!

Remedy for all evil!

Strength of every suff'ring will!

Change what's rotten to Divine,

As was water into wine!

~~

In honor of the Holy Veil of Manoppello
and Sr. Mary of St. Peter.

~

Plays

~

The Light of Faith

This play has been proven by performance.

Characters

Clare: A young girl, 12 – 16, whose lapsed Catholic family has recently moved to Syracuse, New York, to be closer to Clare's older sister, Catherine, whose first baby is almost due. Clare is suffering from an unknown disease and has blurry vision, extreme hunger, and unexplained weight loss. Sweet, but frightened when she begins losing her vision. Her faith gradually strengthens as she learns more about Catholicism. Needs to sing.

Dawn: 11 – 15. Clare's younger sister. Gentle and helpful, but tomboyish. She is scientific and likes to be precise. She loves to learn and to read, which sometimes causes her to for-get her chores. Encourages Clare to be cheerful and studies Catholicism with her. Needs to sing.

Catherine: 16 and older. Clare's 20 year-old married sister, whose first baby is almost due. Joyful, loving, a devout Catholic who tries to revive her family's faith. Preferably should be able to sing for an off-stage piece.

Mother: Was raised with little knowledge of religion and does not understand why anyone would pray to a saint. Does not like the idea of praying to a saint or praying a novena, but is kind and tries to help her daughter accept her crosses. Hard-working and cheerful. Preferably should be able to sing for an off-stage piece.

<u>Father</u>: Hard-working and protective of Clare. A lapsed Catholic, he is not overly eager to become stronger in his Faith, but does not mind if his daughters learn more about it. When he realizes that Clare needs a miracle, he becomes willing to improve himself. Preferably should be able to sing for an off-stage piece.

<u>John:</u> Catherine's husband. Helpful, comical, and a zealous Catholic. Preferably should be able to sing for an off-stage piece.

<u>St. Lucy</u>: As depicted in Swedish traditions – crown or wreath if possible, white gown with red sash. No lines.

<u>Christ Child</u>: Age 5-12. No lines.

<u>Opening Scene:</u>
<u>The New Home</u>

A living room with at least one chair and a small table. Clare, Dawn, and their parents enter, carrying backpacks/suitcases/ other traveling bags.

FATHER: We're here! *(sets down his backpack)*

MOTHER: It certainly was a long drive from New York City.

DAWN: *(dancing around the room)* Four hours and six minutes, to be exact.

CLARE: *(humming)* The flight was about double, I think. *(pulls a granola bar out of her backpack and starts eating it.)*

DAWN: Five minutes *less* than double. You know, for how much you eat, you aren't gaining any weight?

CLARE: *(cheerfully)* I know, but I'm always hungry.

FATHER: It's probably just the excitement of the move.

MOTHER: We had better unpack. We'll start with –

DAWN: Christmas decorations!

CLARE: Why not the Nativity scene, Mom? It's the prettiest decoration we have.

MOTHER: Very well. By the way, Catherine said that she would come over to help us get the house organized. It's certainly nice to be near your sister again, isn't it, girls?

CLARE: Yes, it is. When's her baby due?

MOTHER: *(dusting off the table.)* The end of the month. *(she helps Clare's father set up a Nativity scene)*

DAWN: *(excitedly)* May I unpack my books now?

MOTHER: Go ahead. That reminds me, you girls have to go to school tomorrow. Unpack your school books first.

Dawn and Clare begin pulling books out of their backpacks and putting the school books to the side. Clare pulls out a thesaurus and looks confused.

CLARE: This is a strange dinosaur book. Are we studying dinosaurs in science class, Mother?

MOTHER: *(looking confused)* No, dear, not in Biology.

DAWN: *(gently)* Uh, Clare . . . it actually says "thesaurus."

CLARE: Oh! That makes sense. My eyes are all blurry. *(uncertainly)* I guess I must be tired.

FATHER: As soon as you finish unpacking, you may go and rest.

They hear knocking, the father steps off-stage. He comes back a few moments later with Catherine, who rushes to greet her Mother.

MOTHER: *(surprised and glad)* Catherine! I wasn't expecting you until later.

CATHERINE: I couldn't wait. John is still at work, so I thought I'd come over now. *(turns to greet Clare and Dawn, but stops in surprise.)* Clare, have you lost weight?

CLARE: *(cautiously)* That's strange. I'm always hungry.

CATHERINE: It's probably just the move. You girls will be going to school tomorrow; are you excited?

DAWN: I can't wait! Mother says that it is a really good school, and that they have a great biology class!

CATHERINE: I'm glad you're excited. Well, let's begin unpacking your things.

Second Scene:
Clare's Eyes

The same room. Clare's mother is sitting down, reading a book when Dawn skips in, carrying her backpack and singing a Christmas carol. Clare slowly follows her, holding her schoolbooks. The Mother looks up.

MOTHER: Welcome back! How was school?

DAWN: *(excitedly)* It was great! Remember how we dissected a flower for our Biology class yesterday? Today, we dissected a *worm*! It was *so* neat! Oh, and all the students were given an eye test. I have perfect vision!

MOTHER: Very good! Clare, what about you? How was your day?

CLARE: Oh, the classes were good. I liked the art class best. . . . but they said that my vision is really poor and that I should go to an eye doctor. *(more cheerfully)* I probably just need glasses.

MOTHER: Well, don't worry about it. I'll talk to your father when he gets home, and we'll make an appointment for you. Do you have any homework?

DAWN: Yes, we have do some math and find sources for a research paper. Come on, Clare.

They sit down on a cot on the other side of the stage and begin studying. Their mother starts looking at her phone or reading a book. Clare squints at her paper.

CLARE: Is this page *really* just covered with squiggles?

DAWN: *(concerned)* No . . .

CLARE: *(takes a deep breath)* Would you mind telling me what it says?

DAWN: The Tin Man could chop down ten trees in seven hours. How long would it take him to chop down 39 trees? *(their father walks in)*

FATHER: How was school today?

DAWN: The classes were great, but they gave us an eye test and Clare needs glasses.

FATHER: We had better get you to the eye doctor. Are you able to do your homework?

CLARE: Dawn is reading the problems to me. *(worried)* It seems as if my eyes are worse than they were this morning.

FATHER: Did your mother make an appointment with an eye doctor for you?

MOTHER: I was waiting to talk to you about it, but I have the phone number. I'll call him. *(pretends to dial phone and to have a conversation. Alternatively, after dialing, can exit backstage for the call)*

DAWN: Come on, Clare – how many trees could the Tin Man chop?

CLARE: *(Clare attempts to work the problem on paper, but gives up.)* I can't even see my own writing.

FATHER: Try a magnifying glass. *(gives one to her)*

CLARE: Thanks. *(bends over her paper and works the problem. Her mother hangs up, or if off-stage, re-enters)*

MOTHER: Clare, your appointment is at 2:30 on Saturday. Now, dinner should be almost ready; go and wash up.

The girls get up and turn to exit. Clare trips on Dawn's backpack.

DAWN: *(alarmed)* Watch where you're going, Clare!

CLARE: I *was* watching, but thanks for your concern.

MOTHER: *(sighs)* Hopefully we can get your vision fixed soon. Go along, now.

Dawn picks up her backpack and both girls exit. The lights fade.

Third Scene:
Pray a Novena

A garden. Two chairs and a table covered in a white cloth. Catherine and her Mother are seated there, with John standing next to Catherine.

MOTHER: I'm so glad that we moved to be closer to you. It's been so stressful lately because of Clare's sickness.

JOHN: *(concerned)* Is she feeling worse today?

MOTHER: Her vision is blurrier, and you know that she's been losing weight like crazy even though she can't seem to stop eating. On top of that, the half-mile walk to school completely drains Clare's energy!

CATHERINE: I can't believe that the doctors haven't been able to diagnose her!

MOTHER: I know! The ophthalmologist couldn't help her eyes; the pediatrician has no idea what's wrong with her; and the dietitians, oncologists, and diabetologists we've taken her to have only made suggestions, which haven't helped! Even our prayers seem to be to no avail.

CATHERINE: We should not give up on prayer, Mother.

JOHN: (*enthusiastically*) Exactly! *Never* give up on prayer! It's just like a battle- we keep fighting and we trust in God.

MOTHER: (*sighs*) I know.

JOHN: Where do you attend Mass?

MOTHER: We've been too busy to think about going.

JOHN: (*excited*) Well, we've found this great church, the Basilica of the Sacred Heart! It's beautiful, and there is an amazing Latin Mass on Sunday!

MOTHER: Thanks. We'll look into it, but right now we need to do something for Clare.

CATHERINE: (*touching John's arm*) Hey, John- what about that holy card you picked up for her?

JOHN: Oh, yes! (*pulls a holy card of St. Lucy out of his pocket*)

MOTHER: (*looks at the holy card*) Novena to Saint Lucy, virgin and martyr, the patron saint of eye troubles . . . What's a novena?

CATHERINE: It's nine successive days of prayer, often in the case of an emergency. For us, we are asking St. Lucy to intercede on Clare's behalf, as all our other resources have failed us.

MOTHER: I appreciate your suggestion, but I don't really like the idea of praying to saints because I've heard that it distracts us from God.

JOHN: No, no, no! We pray to God *through* saints! It's part of our faith! A novena is like – like *(struggles to find the right words)* like calling out the National Guard!

MOTHER: *(confused)* The National Guard?

JOHN: Yes, it's like asking a friend to help us when we can't finish a job by ourselves. God does the healing; saints can't do anything that is against God's Will. Therefore, if God *wants* Clare to be healed, she will be. If we trust Him, He will help us to accept His Will over our own. Come on- just give it a try.

CATHERINE: *(coaxingly)* St. Lucy's feast happens to be exactly nine days from now, on December 13. It's a perfect time to pray a novena.

MOTHER: *(looks unconvinced)* I don't know . . .

CATHERINE: Please Mother, just <u>one</u> novena for Clare. *The Father enters on the right.*

FATHER: Did you just say 'novena?'

CATHERINE: *(jumps up to greet him)* Yes, John suggested that we pray a novena for Clare.

FATHER: *(gravely)* That sounds like a 'last resort.' Did you talk to Clare about it?

MOTHER: No, Clare and Dawn are –

Clare and Dawn enter on the left with their schoolbooks.

DAWN: Right here, Mother! *(skips around the table and hugs her)* What did you want us for?

MOTHER: John has something for your sister.

John hands the holy card to Clare, who examines it.

CLARE: What does it say?

JOHN: It has a novena prayer for the intercession of Saint Lucy, a martyr. It is prayed for nine days in the hopes that God will heal you.

FATHER: Are you willing, Clare?

CLARE: Okay. *(She hands the holy card to John. Everyone kneels and makes the Sign of the Cross.*

JOHN: Relying on Thy goodness, O God, we humbly ask Thee, through the intercession of Saint Lucy, virgin and martyr, to give perfect vision to our eyes, that they may serve for Thy greater honor and glory. Saint Lucy, hear our prayers and obtain our petitions. Saint Lucy, please obtain for Clare a complete healing.

CATHERINE: But let God's Most Holy Will be done.

FATHER: We ask this through Christ Our Lord. Amen.

Fourth Scene:
Researching St. Lucy

Clare's family's living room. Clare and Dawn are sitting on the cot, studying. Option A: Their parents are on the left of the stage,. Their father is reading the newspaper and the mother is sewing. Option B: parents are backstage.

DAWN: Well, that's it for math. I think you're doing pretty well, Clare.

CLARE: *(dismally)* It's really hard to do math using a magnifying glass, though.

DAWN: Have you decided what you want to research for your report?

CLARE: *(pauses to think)* Because my eyes are so bad, I won't be able to do the research myself – but I think I'd like to write about Saint Lucy. I guess I should learn more about her since we are praying for her intercession.

Dawn picks up a book about saints. Catherine enters.

DAWN: Catherine!

CATHERINE: Hi! Mom said Clare needs help with her school. How are you, Clare?

CLARE: *(unhappily)* As far as my eyes go, I can barely tell who you are. I think I'm just getting worse.

CATHERINE: *(comfortingly)* Keep praying the novena.

CLARE: *(sighs)* I will.

CATHERINE: Dawn, Mom asked if you remembered to water the flowers this morning.

DAWN: Oops! I forgot. Can you help Clare with her research paper on Saint Lucy? I'll be right back.

CATHERINE: Sure. *(pulls out her phone as Dawn skips off-stage.)*

CLARE: *(uncertainly)* I'm not sure if I'll be able to write anything down.

CATHERINE: Do you have a tape recorder?

Clare rummages in her backpack and holds up a tape recorder.

CATHERINE: Great! You can record while I read to you. *(brief pause)* Let's see . . . Saint Lucy was born around 283

A.D. and was martyred in the year 304. . . She was chaste and never married; instead, she gave away her possessions to the poor.

Dawn skips back in, carrying a book.

CATHERINE: That was fast!

DAWN: Somebody left a glass of water sitting around, so I just dumped it on the flowers. *(sits down next to Clare)* I found a recent translation of a traditional Scandinavian song about Saint Lucy. It's sung on her feast day. *(sings to the tune of the traditional Santa Lucia.)*

> The night falls heavily
> Around the farm and snow.
> Around the earth,
> Shadows are gathering.
> Then in our darkened house
> Arise with lighted crown
> Santa Lucia, Santa Lucia.

CATHERINE: Saint Lucy is also the patron saint of stained-glass workers and writers, just to name a few professions; and she is the patron of Syracuse, Sicily, her home.

CLARE: Is that a coincidence?

CATHERINE: No, dear. I read that the stronger our faith grows, we will see more and more easily how God is working in our lives.

DAWN: Here's a fun tradition from Sweden: on Saint Lucy's feast, the oldest girl in the house wears a robe of white with a red sash, and a crown of lingonberry leaves decorated with candles. Early in the morning, she wakes up everyone else and gives them Saint Lucy bread and coffee.

CLARE: We should do that! Oh . . .wait. I'm the oldest, but you might have to do it, Dawn, if my eyes don't get better. *(puts a hand up to her eyes)*

DAWN: *(looks at Clare and sighs before turning back to her book)* This book says that when Saint Lucy went to distribute her possessions among the poor in the catacombs, she put candles on a crown or wreath, so that her hands would be free.

CATHERINE: Clare, here's a painting of Saint Lucy. *(tries to show Clare, but she is sitting still, staring straight ahead. Worriedly)* Clare? Are you alright?

CLARE: Why is it so dark in here?
Dawn waves a hand in front of Clare's face, but she does not respond.

CLARE: *(Alarmed)* Catherine! What happened?

CATHERINE: Calm down, dear. *(gets up and walks quickly to the left side of the stage. Her parents look up. quietly)* Mom, Dad, Clare is –

DAWN: *(panics and shouts)* <u>BLIND</u>!

CLARE: *(jumps up in shock)* I'm *blind*?!

DAWN: *(leaping about frantically)* Call a doctor! Get an ambulance!

If parents were off-stage, they come running out, Father in front. He grabs Dawn.

FATHER: *(sternly)* Dawn, calm down!

CLARE: *(frightened)* Mother . . . ! *(she collapses in shock and everyone runs to her. Her mother lifts her head into her lap.)*

CATHERINE: I'll call 911. *(quickly pulls out her phone and begins dialing)*

MOTHER: *(anxiously)* Relying on Thy goodness, O God, we humbly ask Thee, through the intercession of Saint Lucy, Thy pure-hearted daughter. . . *(or simply signs herself. Lights fade)*

Fifth Scene:
Clare's Faith and the Vision of Saint Lucy

A hospital room with a cot and a small table with the novena card and a small standing crucifix. Clare is laying down,, praying the novena.

CLARE: . . . To give perfect vision to our eyes, that they may serve for Thy greater honor and glory. Saint Lucy, please obtain for me a complete healing, but if it is not God's Will that I recover, help me to bear my suffering well, and to accomplish His Will for me in all things. Through Christ Our Lord. Amen.

Dawn enters. Clare is startled.

CLARE: Who is it?

DAWN: It's just me, Clare. I'm sorry that you have to be in the hospital. Tomorrow it will have been an entire week! How are you? Is the food okay?

CLARE: I've felt better. *(laughs)* As for the food, it's fine, but the doctor won't let me eat pizza. He's experimenting with diets and he wants me to avoid dairy products. Oh, well! (cheerfully) How were your classes today?

DAWN: (*without enthusiasm*) They were good, but biology wasn't very fun without you. (*penitently*) I still feel awful for causing you to faint.

CLARE: (*kindly*) I probably would have panicked and fainted anyway; please don't worry about it anymore. One good thing about being sick, though, is that I have a lot of time to pray. John taught me about the rosary this morning.

DAWN: Speaking of John, Catherine gave birth to a baby girl just a few hours ago.

CLARE: (*excited*) What's her name?

DAWN: They haven't decided yet.

CLARE: She must be so cute! (*her smile fades. Wistfully*) I hope that I'll be able to see her, but the doctor thinks it'll take a miracle to restore my vision.

DAWN: (*hugs her*) You have to trust in God.

CLARE: I know. I guess what I wish for most of all, is to unite my will to His; that way, I think I could suffer anything, like Saint Lucy.

DAWN: (*sits down next to Clare*) I was thinking that, too . . . She suffered martyrdom for her Faith. We share her Faith, but I don't think we're as strong as she was. I told Mom and Dad that maybe we should thank her for her prayers by promising God that we'll become more faithful.

Their parents enter on the left.

MOTHER: Tomorrow is Saint Lucy's feast; today is the last day of the novena. *(to Dawn)* You had a good idea, Dawn. We'll promise God that we'll do our best to carry out His Will in all things, even if Clare is not healed.

FATHER: Whether or not you are healed, Clare, this suffering is at least part of your path to holiness.

MOTHER: Let's pray.

Everyone but Clare kneels.

FATHER: Dear Saint Lucy, please intercede for us and obtain for Clare the grace of healing, if it be God's Most Holy Will. We ask this through Our Lord Jesus Christ. Amen.

MOTHER: *(lovingly)* You should rest now, Clare.

Clare's parents and Dawn leave. Clare slowly falls asleep, and the lights dim as fog fills the stage. Off-stage, the first two stanzas of Santa Lucia are sung by the remainder of the cast:

Listen! Joy enters
In all the quiet hearts
As if on angel's wings
Saint Lucy pray for us,
Soon will the King of Kings
Come down from Heaven.
Santa Lucia, Santa Lucia!

Saint Lucy appears and kneels, praying. The Christ-Child is beside her. Lucy gestures her petition for Clare; the Christ-Child smiles and stretches His hands towards her. They vanish at the end of the stanza.

The light of faith shines
Banishing the dark of night
She brings us news of life
Christmas is coming nigh;
Christ's star will rise alight
Shine through a rosy sky
Santa Lucia, Santa Lucia.

Clare wakes up. Her eyes widen and she raises her hand, staring in amazement as she realizes that she can see. Wildly she feels objects around her. Arising, she looks upward with a smile and begins to sing joyfully to the melody of "Like the Dawning":

O Saint Lucy,

Daughter of God,
Thou who served Him so faithfully,
How shall I thank thee,
Blessed Lucy?
In song and in prayer,
In joy and sorrow,
I'll mirror thee,
A flame of faith and of purity.

O Saint Lucy,
Pray for us now,
May we adore eternally
The Divine Lamb, our King. Amen.

Alternatively have Clare sing the third stanza of Santa Lucia and the choir only sings the second stanza.

Catherine and John enter quietly. Catherine is holding her baby. Clare's parents and Dawn follow.

FATHER: *(shocked and concerned)* Clare, you shouldn't be up!

Surprised, Clare turns around and smiles. She runs and puts her arms around the baby, shocking her family.

CLARE: I thought I might never get to see you! You're the sweetest, most beautiful baby I ever saw!

MOTHER: *(amazed)* Clare!

DAWN: *(shrieks)* You can *see!*

CLARE: Not only that; I'm sure that I'm completely healed! I saw Saint Lucy praying for me, and Jesus smiled because we trusted in Him! I want to serve Him by becoming an eye doctor. *(to Catherine)* What's your baby's name?

CATHERINE: We named her Lucy.

CLARE: *(gasps)* That's beautiful! I've learned so much about faith from her namesake! Mom, Dad, let's keep our promise and go to Mass!

<u>Sixth Scene:</u>
<u>The Promise is Kept</u>

The living room, decorated for Christmas; the Nativity set is in the center of the table. The family enters on the left while Clare and Dawn playfully sing a carol or the Hallelujah from Handel's Messiah.

MOTHER: What a beautiful Mass!

FATHER: It certainly was! I hadn't attended Midnight Mass for ten years!

DAWN: It was so beautiful, I could have stayed in the basilica for a *million years!*

(her parents laugh. Dawn says sheepishly,) That wasn't very precise. Oh, well!

MOTHER: *(smiling)* Do you know what time it is, girls?

DAWN: It's – um . . . *(glances at her watch)* 2:00.

MOTHER: *(laughing)* Yes, but do you know what it's time for?

DAWN: Time for bed?

MOTHER: No, dear. It's time to place the Christ Child in the manger.

FATHER: And to pray that the faith which has been born in our hearts this December, may burn brightly forever.

The Mother takes a small jewelry box from behind the stable of the Nativity scene. Opening it, she shows the figure of the Christ Child to Dawn and Clare.

MOTHER: You're the youngest, Dawn; you may place Him in the manger.

DAWN: *(hesitates as she takes the box)* I think – I think that Clare should be the one to do it.

Clare, overwhelmed, accepts the box from Dawn and slowly moves to the table. Her parents and Dawn begin singing Silent Night. Clare pauses before the Nativity, then gently removes the image of the Christ Child from the jewelry box. She gazes at Him a moment, reverently kisses Him, and then carefully places Him in the manger.

DAWN: *(softly)* Merry Christmas to us! *(hugs Clare)*

CLARE: *(turning to look at the manger)* And Happy Birthday to Thee, Jesus!

They join their parents and finish singing Silent Night together.

THE END

Saint Francis and

the Tradition of the Creche

This play has been proven by performance.

Characters

Saint Francis- Joyful, prayerful, feels strong emotion when meditating on the Birth of Christ.

St. Bonaventure (BV) – a scholarly, pious Franciscan who lived in the time of St. Francis

Sir John of Velita – Lord of Greccio, a brave soldier and an obedient, willing helper of St. Francis.

Pope Honorius III – Dignified, glad to help St. Francis.

Alticama: Sir John's gentle bride. She makes the image of the Christ Child for the manger.

Messenger: 8 – 14. Only has lines in the second scene, but could be present in the fifth scene. If it is played by a girl, it could be Alticama.

<u>Opening Scene:</u>

One side of the stage has a desk, and possibly a crucifix. St. Bonaventure is writing at the left side of the stage, but gets up after a moment and begins walking slowly about as he reads what he has written. He looks up and addresses the audience:

BV: Good morning/afternoon/evening! My name is Bonaventure. I am recording the life of the holy founder of my order, St. Francis of Assisi. You may know that he began the tradition of the Nativity scene; but do you know the whole story? In 1223, three years before his death, St. Francis made a pilgrimage to the Holy Land. When he came to the Basilica of the Nativity, he entered and made his way down to the Grotto, where Jesus Our Lord was born of the Virgin Mary one-thousand years and two centuries ago . . .

Lights switch to the rest of the stage, showing the Cave of the Nativity in Bethlehem. Francis enters on the right and kneels before the silver star that marks the place of Jesus' birth. While he is meditating, the lights dim and "Away In A Manger" is sung quietly while those playing the Holy Family take their places. Mary holds the Infant as she kneels at the star. The lights brighten and Francis looks up, surprised, and gazes at the scene.

FRANCIS: Now I see His poverty! *(astonished)* If only all could understand the infinite love that made Him descend from Heaven! *(He begins singing St. Alphonsus Ligouri's "From Starry Skies Thou Comest")*:

> From starry skies descending,
> Thou comest, glorious King,
> A manger low Thy bed,
> In winter's icy sting;
> O my dearest Child most holy,
> Shudd'ring, trembling in the cold!
> Great God, Thou lovest me!
> What suff'ring Thou didst bear,
> That I near Thee might be!
>
> Thou art the world's Creator,
> God's own and true Word,
> Yet here no robe, no fire
> For Thee, Divine Lord.
> Dearest, fairest, sweetest Infant,
> Dire this state of poverty.
> The more I care for Thee,
> Since Thou, O Love Divine,
> Will'st now so poor to be.

The lights fade.

Second Scene:
The Invitation

Francis is slowly walking across the stage from the left, carrying a staff, and meets a young boy, who is walking from the right. Half of the stage remains dark, so that when Francis begins walking again, the third scene may begin immediately.

FRANCIS: May God bless you, son!

MESSENGER: Brother Francis?

FRANCIS: Yes?

MESSENGER: I bring you a letter from Greccio. *(Francis takes the letter and reads it.)*

FRANCIS: *(to himself)* They invite me to join them for Midnight Mass on Christmas. Greccio! It is a beautiful place. *(to the boy)* Tell them that I will come.

The boy bows and exits on the right. Francis begins to pray silently and BV begins to speak.

Third Scene:
St. Francis and the Pope

BV: Francis was determined to keep the feast of the Nativity with all possible solemnity, hoping to deepen the devotion of the people of Greccio. He planned to create a living Nativity scene for them. In the past, however, similar Christmas celebrations had become irreverent and had been forbidden by the Holy Father. Thus, Francis knew that he needed to return to Rome to obtain permission.

Francis begins walking, and the right side of the stage is lit up to show a garden or a room at the Vatican suitable for Pope Honorius III to receive him in.

FRANCIS: May God bless you, Your Holiness! *(Joyfully stoops and kisses the Pope's ring)*

THE POPE: God's blessings upon you, Brother Francis. How are you?

FRANCIS: As well as God wishes me to be. I have just returned from Bethlehem.

THE POPE: Ah! *(He and Francis begin strolling across the stage, then pause.)*

FRANCIS: When I saw the place where the Babe was laid in a manger, I felt moved to recreate it.

Pope looks concerned and thoughtfully turns and moves away on the right, and then stops as Francis, eagerly continues:

FRANCIS: Holy Father, will you permit it?

THE POPE: (seriously) You know that in the past, Brother Francis, such Christmas ceremonies have moved from veneration to irreverence. I had to forbid them years ago.

FRANCIS: *(humbly)* I am well aware of it, Holy Father. I do not wish to be irreverent. I hope that the people will become more devoted to the Christ-Child by seeing, in a way, the difficulties surrounding His birth.

The Pope has been looking at him thoughtfully, and then deciding to trust him, approaches.

THE POPE: I trust you, Brother Francis. I give you, and your work, my blessing.

Raising his hand, he makes the Sign of the Cross over Francis, who kneels.

THE POPE: Now I must attend to my duties. May God bless you, Brother Francis.

The Pope exits on the left of the stage. A bell tolls. Francis pauses, makes the Sign of the Cross and prays for a moment, before exiting on the right. Again the lights fade.

BV: Thus, filled with the joy of God's blessings, Francis proceeded to the home of his good friend, Sir John of Velita, Lord of Greccio, to beg his help in realizing his plans.

Fourth Scene:
Meeting Sir John of Velita

Christmas Eve. A scene suitable for portraying a nobleman's home, with at least one chair, and a small table. A servant leads Francis in. Alticama is seated in the chair, sewing or reading. Sir John can either be practicing his skill with a blade or pacing while reading. (The sword was found to be popular with the audience.) Sir John looks up.

BV: Sir John was a valiant and veracious soldier, who, for the love of Christ, had left the warfare of this world and become a dear friend of Francis'. When the Saint arrived at the nobleman's home, he found both Sir John and Alticama, his bride, eager to help him.

SIR JOHN: *(overjoyed, moving to greet him)* Brother Francis! What brings you to my unworthy house this Christmas Eve?

FRANCIS: May God bless you, Sir John, and your wife. I come to beg a favor of you.

SIR JOHN: Anything to glorify God!

FRANCIS: I have just returned from the Holy Land, where I visited the birthplace of Christ; how I desire that all might see and understand His poverty!

SIR JOHN: But you have an idea?

FRANCIS: *(slowly)* I have been invited to Midnight Mass here in Greccio. *(eagerly)* I wish to do something that will recall the memory of the little Child Who was born in Bethlehem, to see the inconveniences of His infancy, how He lay in the manger, and how the ox and ass stood by.

SIR JOHN: *(surprised)* That is unusual!

FRANCIS: But I do it not for lightness or novelty, John; I hope to deepen the people's devotion. The Holy Father has given it his blessing. Will you help me?

SIR JOHN: Right willingly!

ALTICAMA: *(Optional. Arises, possibly dropping her sewing/book and says eagerly)* Please, Brother Francis; will you allow me to create an image of the Christ-Child for the manger?

FRANCIS: Gladly! Sir John, may I beg your help in making everything ready?

SIR JOHN: Certainly!

Francis and John exit on the right.

Fifth Scene:
Preparing the Manger and
Celebrating Midnight Mass

A cave-like setting. In the center of the stage is a table to serve as an altar. Sir John and Francis are "finishing up" a manger on the far right.

BV: Francis helped Sir John prepare a manger, and brought hay and an ox and an ass to the place appointed. . .

Francis gathers some hay from a pile and places it in the manger. John brings a cardboard drawing of an ox while Francis brings the ass.; or, children dressed as an ox and a donkey.

A girl playing Mary and a boy playing Joseph take their places, with Mary kneeling beside the manger and Joseph standing at the head of the manger, holding a lantern.

Optional: Alticama enters, cradling the image of the Christ-Child, which may be bundled up, and places it reverently in the manger).

BV: Then the brethren were summoned, the people ran together-

Several Franciscan brothers enter on the left, possibly holding candles, the townspeople, taken from the audience if possible, follow the brothers.

BV: The forest resounded with their voices, and that venerable night was made glorious by many brilliant lights and psalms of praise. Midnight Mass was said, and Francis joyfully served as deacon. That Christmas night, the Holy Gospel was chanted by Francis, the Levite of Christ.

Francis has been pantomiming as BV speaks, but now reads:

FRANCIS: *(emotionally)* …. "and they laid Him in a manger…"

He kneels in front of the manger. The lights dim and a single light slowly illuminates the manger as people behind the curtain begin softly singing "Silent Night."

BV: Sir John affirmed that he beheld a beautiful Infant sleeping in the manger, Whom the blessed Father Francis embraced as if he would wake Him from sleep.

If Alticama does not make the image of the Infant, in the brief pause between the dimming of the main lights and the illuminating of the manger, Mary places an image of the Christ

Child in it. Francis embraces the Infant. Slowly the light on the manger dims and the singing fades.

Closing Scene:
The Tradition

BV: *(seriously)* The vision of the Christ Child is credible, not only because of the sanctity of Sir John, but because of the miracles that afterward confirmed it. For, the hay of that manger miraculously cured animals and helped women with difficult births; God thus glorified His servant and witnessed to the great efficacy of his prayers. Thus began the tradition of the Nativity scene.

Option A: Children representing different countries process across the stage, carrying a flag. They sing one or more stanzas of "Away in a Manger." BV joins them as they make their way across the stage, where Francis is kneeling beside the manger. The children and BV kneel to pray.

Option B: Same, but instead it's the actors of the play, and no flags.

THE END

www.ingramcontent.com/pod-product-compliance
Lightning Source LLC
LaVergne TN
LVHW051425080426
835508LV00022B/3250